UNCLE VANYA

Scenes from Country Life; A Drama in Four Acts

ANTON CHEKHOV

Translated by
MARIAN FELL

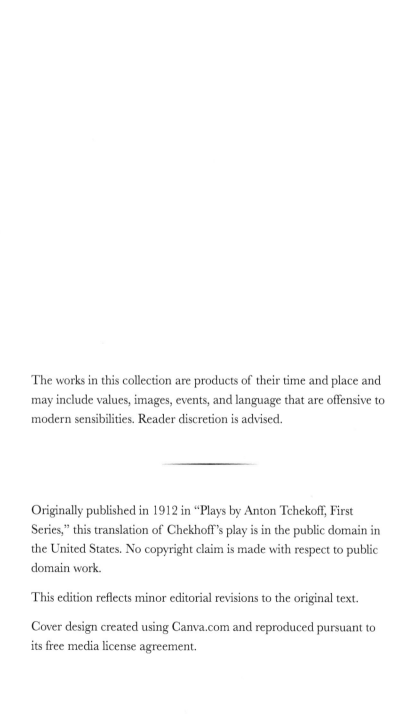

CONTENTS

CHARACTERS

ALEXANDER SEREBRAKOFF, a retired professor

HELENA, his wife, twenty-seven years old

SONIA, his daughter by a former marriage

MME. VOITSKAYA, widow of a privy councilor, and mother of Serebrakoff's first wife

IVAN (VANYA) VOITSKI, her son

MICHAEL ASTROFF, a doctor

ILIA (WAFFLES) TELEGIN, an impoverished landowner

MARINA, an old nurse

A WORKMAN

The scene is laid on SEREBRAKOFF'S country place

ACT I

[A country house on a terrace. In front of it a garden. In an avenue of trees, under an old poplar, stands a table set for tea, with a samovar, etc. Some benches and chairs stand near the table. On one of them is lying a guitar. A hammock is swung near the table. It is three o'clock in the afternoon of a cloudy day.]

[MARINA, a quiet, grey-haired, little old woman, is sitting at the table knitting a stocking.]

[ASTROFF is walking up and down near her.]

MARINA. *[Pouring some tea into a glass]* Take a little tea, my son.

ASTROFF. *[Takes the glass from her unwillingly]* Somehow, I don't seem to want any.

MARINA. Then will you have a little vodka instead?

ASTROFF. No, I don't drink vodka every day, and besides, it is too hot now. *[A pause]* Tell me, nurse, how long have we known each other?

MARINA. *[Thoughtfully]* Let me see, how long is it? Lord—help me to remember. You first came here, into our parts—let me think—when was it? Sonia's mother was still alive—it was two winters before she died; that was eleven years ago—*[thoughtfully]* perhaps more.

ASTROFF. Have I changed much since then?

MARINA. Oh, yes. You were handsome and young then, and now you are an old man and not handsome any more. You drink, too.

ASTROFF. Yes, ten years have made me another man. And why? Because I am overworked. Nurse, I am on my feet from dawn till dusk. I know no rest; at night I tremble under my blankets for fear of being dragged out to visit some one who is sick; I have toiled without repose or a day's freedom since I have known you; could I help growing old? And then, existence is tedious, anyway; it is a senseless, dirty business, this life, and goes heavily. Every one about here is silly, and after living with them for two or three years one grows silly oneself. It is inevitable. *[Twisting his moustache]* See what a long moustache I have grown. A foolish, long moustache. Yes, I am as silly as the rest, nurse, but not as stupid; no, I have not grown stupid. Thank God, my brain is not addled yet, though my feelings have grown numb. I ask nothing, I need nothing, I love no one, unless it is yourself alone. *[He kisses her head]* I had a nurse just like you when I was a child.

MARINA. Don't you want a bite of something to eat?

ASTROFF. No. During the third week of Lent I went to the epidemic at Malitskoi. It was eruptive typhoid. The peasants were all lying side by side in their huts, and the calves and pigs were running about the floor among the sick. Such dirt there was, and smoke! Unspeakable! I slaved among those people all day, not a crumb passed my lips, but when I got home there was still no rest for me; a switchman was carried in from the railroad; I laid him on the operating table and he went and died in my arms under chloroform, and then my feelings that should have been deadened awoke again, my conscience tortured me as if I had killed the man. I sat down and closed my eyes—like this—and thought: will our descendants two hundred years from now, for whom we are breaking the road, remember to give us a kind word? No, nurse, they will forget.

MARINA. Man is forgetful, but God remembers.

ASTROFF. Thank you for that. You have spoken the truth.

Enter VOITSKI from the house. He has been asleep after dinner and looks rather dishevelled. He sits down on the bench and straightens his collar.

VOITSKI. H'm. Yes. *[A pause]* Yes.

ASTROFF. Have you been asleep?

VOITSKI. Yes, very much so. *[He yawns]* Ever since the Professor and his wife have come, our daily life seems to have jumped the track. I sleep at the wrong time, drink wine, and eat all sorts of messes for luncheon and dinner. It isn't wholesome. Sonia and I used to work together and never had an idle moment, but now Sonia works alone and I only eat and drink and sleep. Something is wrong.

MARINA. *[Shaking her head]* Such a confusion in the house! The Professor gets up at twelve, the samovar is kept boiling all the morning, and everything has to wait for him. Before they came we used to have dinner at one o'clock, like everybody else, but now we have it at seven. The Professor sits up all night writing and reading, and suddenly, at two o'clock, there goes the bell! Heavens, what is that? The Professor wants some tea! Wake the servants, light the samovar! Lord, what disorder!

ASTROFF. Will they be here long?

VOITSKI. A hundred years! The Professor has decided to make his home here.

MARINA. Look at this now! The samovar has been on the table for two hours, and they are all out walking!

VOITSKI. All right, don't get excited; here they come.

[Voices are heard approaching. SEREBRAKOFF, HELENA, SONIA, and TELEGIN come in from the depths of the garden, returning from their walk.]

SEREBRAKOFF. Superb! Superb! What beautiful views!

TELEGIN. They are wonderful, your Excellency.

SONIA. To-morrow we shall go into the woods, shall we, papa?

VOITSKI. Ladies and gentlemen, tea is ready.

SEREBRAKOFF. Won't you please be good enough to send my tea into the library? I still have some work to finish.

SONIA. I am sure you will love the woods.

HELENA, SEREBRAKOFF, and SONIA go into the house. TELEGIN sits down at the table beside MARINA.

VOITSKI. There goes our learned scholar on a hot, sultry day like this, in his overcoat and goloshes and carrying an umbrella!

ASTROFF. He is trying to take good care of his health.

VOITSKI. How lovely she is! How lovely! I have never in my life seen a more beautiful woman.

TELEGIN. Do you know, Marina, that as I walk in the fields or in the shady garden, as I look at this table here, my heart swells with unbounded happiness. The weather is enchanting, the birds are singing, we are all living in peace and contentment—what more could the soul desire? *[Takes a glass of tea.]*

VOITSKI. *[Dreaming]* Such eyes—a glorious woman!

ASTROFF. Come, Ivan, tell us something.

VOITSKI. *[Indolently]* What shall I tell you?

ASTROFF. Haven't you any news for us?

VOITSKI. No, it is all stale. I am just the same as usual, or perhaps worse, because I have become lazy. I don't do anything now but croak like an old raven. My mother, the old magpie, is still chattering about the emancipation of woman, with one eye on her grave and the other on her learned books, in which she is always looking for the dawn of a new life.

ASTROFF. And the Professor?

VOITSKI. The Professor sits in his library from morning till night, as usual—

> "Straining the mind, wrinkling the
>   brow,
> We write, write, write,
> Without respite
> Or hope of praise in the future or now."

Poor paper! He ought to write his autobiography; he would make a really splendid subject for a book! Imagine it, the life of a retired professor, as stale as a piece of hardtack, tortured by gout, headaches, and rheumatism, his liver bursting with jealousy and envy, living on the estate of his first wife, although he hates it, because he can't afford to live in town. He is everlastingly whining about his hard lot, though, as a matter of fact, he is extraordinarily lucky. He is the son of a common deacon and has attained the professor's chair, become the son-in-law of a senator, is called "your Excellency," and so on. But I'll tell you something; the man has been writing on art for twenty-five years, and he doesn't know the very first thing about it. For twenty-five years he has been chewing on other men's thoughts about realism, naturalism, and all such foolishness; for twenty-five years he has been reading and writing things that clever men have long known and stupid ones are not interested in; for twenty-five years he has been making his imaginary mountains out of molehills. And just think of the man's self-conceit and presumption all this time! For twenty-five years he has been masquerading in false clothes and has now retired absolutely unknown to any living soul; and yet see him! stalking across the earth like a demi-god!

ASTROFF. I believe you envy him.

VOITSKI. Yes, I do. Look at the success he has had with women! Don Juan himself was not more favoured. His first wife, who was my sister, was a beautiful, gentle being, as pure as the blue heaven there above us, noble, great-hearted, with more admirers than he has pupils, and she loved him as only beings of angelic purity can love those who are as pure and beautiful as themselves. His mother-in-law, my mother, adores him to this day, and he still inspires a sort of worshipful awe in her. His second wife is, as you see, a brilliant beauty; she married him in his old age and has surrendered all the glory of her beauty and freedom to him. Why? What for?

ASTROFF. Is she faithful to him?

VOITSKI. Yes, unfortunately she is.

ASTROFF. Why unfortunately?

VOITSKI. Because such fidelity is false and unnatural, root and branch. It sounds well, but there is no logic in it. It is thought immoral for a woman to deceive an old husband whom she hates, but quite moral for her to strangle her poor youth in her breast and banish every vital desire from her heart.

TELEGIN. *[In a tearful voice]* Vanya, I don't like to hear you talk so. Listen, Vanya; every one who betrays husband or wife is faithless, and could also betray his country.

VOITSKI. *[Crossly]* Turn off the tap, Waffles.

TELEGIN. No, allow me, Vanya. My wife ran away with a lover on the day after our wedding, because my exterior was unprepossessing. I have never failed in my duty since then. I love her and am true to her to this day. I help her all I can and have given my fortune to educate the daughter of herself and her lover. I have forfeited my happiness, but I have kept my pride. And she? Her youth has fled, her beauty has faded according to the laws of nature, and her lover is dead. What has she kept?

HELENA and SONIA come in; after them comes MME. VOITSKAYA carrying a book. She sits down and begins to read. Some one hands her a glass of tea which she drinks without looking up.

SONIA. *[Hurriedly, to the nurse]* There are some peasants waiting out there. Go and see what they want. I shall pour the tea. *[Pours out some glasses of tea.]*

MARINA goes out. HELENA takes a glass and sits drinking in the hammock.

ASTROFF. I have come to see your husband. You wrote me that he had rheumatism and I know not what else, and that he was very ill, but he appears to be as lively as a cricket.

HELENA. He had a fit of the blues yesterday evening and complained of pains in his legs, but he seems all right again to-day.

ASTROFF. And I galloped over here twenty miles at break-neck speed! No matter, though, it is not the first time. Once here, however, I am going to stay until to-morrow, and at any rate sleep *quantum satis.*

SONIA. Oh, splendid! You so seldom spend the night with us. Have you had dinner yet?

ASTROFF. No.

SONIA. Good. So you will have it with us. We dine at seven now. *[Drinks her tea]* This tea is cold!

TELEGIN. Yes, the samovar has grown cold.

HELENA. Don't mind, Monsieur Ivan, we will drink cold tea, then.

TELEGIN. I beg your pardon, my name is not Ivan, but Ilia, ma'am—Ilia Telegin, or Waffles, as I am sometimes called on account of my pock-marked face. I am Sonia's godfather, and his Excellency, your husband, knows me very well. I now live with you, ma'am, on this estate, and perhaps you will be so good as to notice that I dine with you every day.

SONIA. He is our great help, our right-hand man. *[Tenderly]* Dear godfather, let me pour you some tea.

MME. VOITSKAYA. Oh! Oh!

SONIA. What is it, grandmother?

MME. VOITSKAYA. I forgot to tell Alexander—I have lost my memory—I received a letter to-day from Paul Alexevitch in Kharkoff. He has sent me a new pamphlet.

ASTROFF. Is it interesting?

MME. VOITSKAYA. Yes, but strange. He refutes the very theories which he defended seven years ago. It is appalling!

VOITSKI. There is nothing appalling about it. Drink your tea, mamma.

MME. VOITSKAYA. It seems you never want to listen to what I have to say. Pardon me, Jean, but you have changed so in the last year that I hardly know you. You used to be a man of settled convictions and had an illuminating personality——

VOITSKI. Oh, yes. I had an illuminating personality, which illuminated no one. *[A pause]* I had an illuminating personality! You couldn't say anything more biting. I am forty-seven years old. Until last year I endeavoured, as you do now, to blind my eyes by your pedantry to the truths of life. But now—Oh, if you only knew! If you knew how I lie awake at night, heartsick and angry, to think how stupidly I have wasted my time when I might have been winning from life everything which my old age now forbids.

SONIA. Uncle Vanya, how dreary!

MME. VOITSKAYA. *[To her son]* You speak as if your former convictions were somehow to blame, but you yourself, not they, were at fault. You have forgotten that a conviction, in itself, is nothing but a dead letter. You should have done something.

VOITSKI. Done something! Not every man is capable of being a writer *perpetuum mobile* like your Herr Professor.

MME. VOITSKAYA. What do you mean by that?

SONIA. *[Imploringly]* Mother! Uncle Vanya! I entreat you!

VOITSKI. I am silent. I apologise and am silent. *[A pause.]*

HELENA. What a fine day! Not too hot. *[A pause.]*

VOITSKI. A fine day to hang oneself.

TELEGIN tunes the guitar. MARINA appears near the house, calling the chickens.

MARINA. Chick, chick, chick!

SONIA. What did the peasants want, nurse?

MARINA. The same old thing, the same old nonsense. Chick, chick, chick!

SONIA. Why are you calling the chickens?

MARINA. The speckled hen has disappeared with her chicks. I am afraid the crows have got her.

TELEGIN plays a polka. All listen in silence. Enter WORKMAN.

WORKMAN. Is the doctor here? *[To ASTROFF]* Excuse me, sir, but I have been sent to fetch you.

ASTROFF. Where are you from?

WORKMAN. The factory.

ASTROFF. *[Annoyed]* Thank you. There is nothing for it, then, but to go. *[Looking around him for his cap]* Damn it, this is annoying!

SONIA. Yes, it is too bad, really. You must come back to dinner from the factory.

ASTROFF. No, I won't be able to do that. It will be too late. Now where, where—*[To the WORKMAN]* Look here, my man, get me a glass of vodka, will you? *[The*

WORKMAN goes out] Where—where—*[Finds his cap]* One of the characters in Ostroff's plays is a man with a long moustache and short wits, like me. However, let me bid you good-bye, ladies and gentlemen. *[To HELENA]* I should be really delighted if you would come to see me some day with Miss Sonia. My estate is small, but if you are interested in such things I should like to show you a nursery and seed-bed whose like you will not find within a thousand miles of here. My place is surrounded by government forests. The forester is old and always ailing, so I superintend almost all the work myself.

HELENA. I have always heard that you were very fond of the woods. Of course one can do a great deal of good by helping to preserve them, but does not that work interfere with your real calling?

ASTROFF. God alone knows what a man's real calling is.

HELENA. And do you find it interesting?

ASTROFF. Yes, very.

VOITSKI. *[Sarcastically]* Oh, extremely!

HELENA. You are still young, not over thirty-six or seven, I should say, and I suspect that the woods do not

interest you as much as you say they do. I should think
you would find them monotonous.

SONIA. No, the work is thrilling. Dr. Astroff watches
over the old woods and sets out new plantations every
year, and he has already received a diploma and a
bronze medal. If you will listen to what he can tell you,
you will agree with him entirely. He says that forests are
the ornaments of the earth, that they teach mankind to
understand beauty and attune his mind to lofty
sentiments. Forests temper a stern climate, and in
countries where the climate is milder, less strength is
wasted in the battle with nature, and the people are
kind and gentle. The inhabitants of such countries are
handsome, tractable, sensitive, graceful in speech and
gesture. Their philosophy is joyous, art and science
blossom among them, their treatment of women is full
of exquisite nobility——

VOITSKI. [Laughing] Bravo! Bravo! All that is very
pretty, but it is also unconvincing. So, my friend [To
ASTROFF] you must let me go on burning firewood in
my stoves and building my sheds of planks.

ASTROFF. You can burn peat in your stoves and build
your sheds of stone. Oh, I don't object, of course, to
cutting wood from necessity, but why destroy the
forests? The woods of Russia are trembling under the

blows of the axe. Millions of trees have perished. The homes of the wild animals and birds have been desolated; the rivers are shrinking, and many beautiful landscapes are gone forever. And why? Because men are too lazy and stupid to stoop down and pick up their fuel from the ground. *[To HELENA]* Am I not right, Madame? Who but a stupid barbarian could burn so much beauty in his stove and destroy that which he cannot make? Man is endowed with reason and the power to create, so that he may increase that which has been given him, but until now he has not created, but demolished. The forests are disappearing, the rivers are running dry, the game is exterminated, the climate is spoiled, and the earth becomes poorer and uglier every day. *[To VOITSKI]* I read irony in your eye; you do not take what I am saying seriously, and—and—after all, it may very well be nonsense. But when I pass peasant-forests that I have preserved from the axe, or hear the rustling of the young plantations set out with my own hands, I feel as if I had had some small share in improving the climate, and that if mankind is happy a thousand years from now I will have been a little bit responsible for their happiness. When I plant a little birch tree and then see it budding into young green and swaying in the wind, my heart swells with pride and I —*[Sees the WORKMAN, who is bringing him a glass of vodka on a tray]* however—*[He drinks]* I must be off. Probably it is all nonsense, anyway. Good-bye.

[He goes toward the house. SONIA takes his arm and goes with him.]

SONIA. When are you coming to see us again?

ASTROFF. I can't say.

SONIA. In a month?

[ASTROFF and SONIA go into the house. HELENA and VOITSKI walk over to the terrace.]

HELENA. You have behaved shockingly again. Ivan, what sense was there in teasing your mother and talking about *perpetuum mobile?* And at breakfast you quarreled with Alexander again. Really, your behaviour is too petty.

VOITSKI. But if I hate him?

HELENA. You hate Alexander without reason; he is like every one else, and no worse than you are.

VOITSKI. If you could only see your face, your gestures! Oh, how tedious your life must be.

HELENA. It is tedious, yes, and dreary! You all abuse my husband and look on me with compassion; you think, "Poor woman, she is married to an old man." How well I understand your compassion! As Astroff said just now, see how you thoughtlessly destroy the forests, so that there will soon be none left. So you also destroy mankind, and soon fidelity and purity and self-sacrifice will have vanished with the woods. Why cannot you look calmly at a woman unless she is yours? Because, the doctor was right, you are all possessed by a devil of destruction; you have no mercy on the woods or the birds or on women or on one another.

VOITSKI. I don't like your philosophy.

HELENA. That doctor has a sensitive, weary face—an interesting face. Sonia evidently likes him, and she is in love with him, and I can understand it. This is the third time he has been here since I have come, and I have not had a real talk with him yet or made much of him. He thinks I am disagreeable. Do you know, Ivan, the reason you and I are such friends? I think it is because we are both lonely and unfortunate. Yes, unfortunate. Don't look at me in that way, I don't like it.

VOITSKI. How can I look at you otherwise when I love you? You are my joy, my life, and my youth. I know that my chances of being loved in return are infinitely small, do not exist, but I ask nothing of you. Only let me look at you, listen to your voice—

HELENA. Hush, some one will overhear you.

[They go toward the house.]

VOITSKI. *[Following her]* Let me speak to you of my love, do not drive me away, and this alone will be my greatest happiness!

HELENA. Ah! This is agony!

TELEGIN strikes the strings of his guitar and plays a polka. MME. VOITSKAYA writes something on the leaves of her pamphlet.

The curtain falls.

[The dining-room of SEREBRAKOFF'S house. It is night. The tapping of the WATCHMAN'S rattle is heard in the garden. SEREBRAKOFF is dozing in an arm-chair by an open window and HELENA is sitting beside him, also half asleep.]

SEREBRAKOFF. *[Rousing himself]* Who is here? Is it you, Sonia?

HELENA. It is I.

SEREBRAKOFF. Oh, it is you, Nelly. This pain is intolerable.

HELENA. Your shawl has slipped down. *[She wraps up his legs in the shawl]* Let me shut the window.

SEREBRAKOFF. No, leave it open; I am suffocating. I dreamt just now that my left leg belonged to some one else, and it hurt so that I woke. I don't believe this is gout, it is more like rheumatism. What time is it?

HELENA. Half past twelve. *[A pause.]*

SEREBRAKOFF. I want you to look for Batushka's works in the library to-morrow. I think we have him.

HELENA. What is that?

SEREBRAKOFF. Look for Batushka to-morrow morning; we used to have him, I remember. Why do I find it so hard to breathe?

HELENA. You are tired; this is the second night you have had no sleep.

SEREBRAKOFF. They say that Turgenieff got angina of the heart from gout. I am afraid I am getting angina too. Oh, damn this horrible, accursed old age! Ever since I have been old I have been hateful to myself, and I am sure, hateful to you all as well.

HELENA. You speak as if we were to blame for your being old.

SEREBRAKOFF. I am more hateful to you than to any one.

HELENA gets up and walks away from him, sitting down at a distance.

SEREBRAKOFF. You are quite right, of course. I am not an idiot; I can understand you. You are young and healthy and beautiful, and longing for life, and I am an old dotard, almost a dead man already. Don't I know it? Of course I see that it is foolish for me to live so long, but wait! I shall soon set you all free. My life cannot drag on much longer.

HELENA. You are overtaxing my powers of endurance. Be quiet, for God's sake!

SEREBRAKOFF. It appears that, thanks to me, everybody's power of endurance is being overtaxed; everybody is miserable, only I am blissfully triumphant. Oh, yes, of course!

HELENA. Be quiet! You are torturing me.

SEREBRAKOFF. I torture everybody. Of course.

HELENA. [Weeping] This is unbearable! Tell me, what is it you want me to do?

SEREBRAKOFF. Nothing.

HELENA. Then be quiet, please.

SEREBRAKOFF. It is funny that everybody listens to Ivan and his old idiot of a mother, but the moment I open my lips you all begin to feel ill-treated. You can't even stand the sound of my voice. Even if I am hateful, even if I am a selfish tyrant, haven't I the right to be one at my age? Haven't I deserved it? Haven't I, I ask you, the right to be respected, now that I am old?

HELENA. No one is disputing your rights. *[The window slams in the wind]* The wind is rising, I must shut the window. *[She shuts it]* We shall have rain in a moment. Your rights have never been questioned by anybody.

[The WATCHMAN in the garden sounds his rattle.]

SEREBRAKOFF. I have spent my life working in the interests of learning. I am used to my library and the lecture hall and to the esteem and admiration of my colleagues. Now I suddenly find myself plunged in this wilderness, condemned to see the same stupid people from morning till night and listen to their futile conversation. I want to live; I long for success and fame and the stir of the world, and here I am in exile! Oh, it is dreadful to spend every moment grieving for the lost past, to see the success of others and sit here with nothing to do but to fear death. I cannot stand it! It is more than I can bear. And you will not even forgive me for being old!

HELENA. Wait, have patience; I shall be old myself in four or five years.

[SONIA comes in.]

SONIA. Father, you sent for Dr. Astroff, and now when he comes you refuse to see him. It is not nice to give a man so much trouble for nothing.

SEREBRAKOFF. What do I care about your Astroff? He understands medicine about as well as I understand astronomy.

SONIA. We can't send for the whole medical faculty, can we, to treat your gout?

SEREBRAKOFF. I won't talk to that madman!

SONIA. Do as you please. It's all the same to me. *[She sits down.]*

SEREBRAKOFF. What time is it?

HELENA. One o'clock.

SEREBRAKOFF. It is stifling in here. Sonia, hand me that bottle on the table.

SONIA. Here it is. *[She hands him a bottle of medicine.]*

SEREBRAKOFF. *[Crossly]* No, not that one! Can't you understand me? Can't I ask you to do a thing?

SONIA. Please don't be captious with me. Some people may like it, but you must spare me, if you please, because I don't. Besides, I haven't the time; we are cutting the hay to-morrow and I must get up early.

[VOITSKI comes in dressed in a long gown and carrying a candle.]

VOITSKI. A thunderstorm is coming up. *[The lightning flashes]* There it is! Go to bed, Helena and Sonia. I have come to take your place.

SEREBRAKOFF. *[Frightened]* No, n-o, no! Don't leave me alone with him! Oh, don't. He will begin to lecture me.

VOITSKI. But you must give them a little rest. They have not slept for two nights.

SEREBRAKOFF. Then let them go to bed, but you go away too! Thank you. I implore you to go. For the sake of our former friendship do not protest against going. We will talk some other time——

VOITSKI. Our former friendship! Our former——

SONIA. Hush, Uncle Vanya!

SEREBRAKOFF. *[To his wife]* My darling, don't leave me alone with him. He will begin to lecture me.

VOITSKI. This is ridiculous.

[MARINA comes in carrying a candle.]

SONIA. You must go to bed, nurse, it is late.

MARINA. I haven't cleared away the tea things. Can't go to bed yet.

SEREBRAKOFF. No one can go to bed. They are all worn out, only I enjoy perfect happiness.

MARINA. *[Goes up to SEREBRAKOFF and speaks tenderly]* What's the matter, master? Does it hurt? My own legs are aching too, oh, so badly. *[Arranges his shawl about his legs]* You have had this illness such a long time. Sonia's dead mother used to stay awake with you too, and wear herself out for you. She loved you dearly. *[A pause]* Old people want to be pitied as much as young ones, but nobody cares about them somehow. *[She kisses SEREBRAKOFF'S shoulder]* Come, master, let me give you some linden-tea and warm your poor feet for you. I shall pray to God for you.

SEREBRAKOFF. *[Touched]* Let us go, Marina.

MARINA. My own feet are aching so badly, oh, so badly! *[She and SONIA lead SEREBRAKOFF out]* Sonia's mother used to wear herself out with sorrow and weeping. You were still little and foolish then, Sonia. Come, come, master.

[SEREBRAKOFF, SONIA and MARINA go out.]

HELENA. I am absolutely exhausted by him, and can hardly stand.

VOITSKI. You are exhausted by him, and I am exhausted by my own self. I have not slept for three nights.

HELENA. Something is wrong in this house. Your mother hates everything but her pamphlets and the professor; the professor is vexed, he won't trust me, and fears you; Sonia is angry with her father, and with me, and hasn't spoken to me for two weeks; I am at the end of my strength, and have come near bursting into tears at least twenty times to-day. Something is wrong in this house.

VOITSKI. Leave speculating alone.

HELENA. You are cultured and intelligent, Ivan, and you surely understand that the world is not destroyed by villains and conflagrations, but by hate and malice and all this spiteful tattling. It is your duty to make peace, and not to growl at everything.

VOITSKI. Help me first to make peace with myself. My darling! *[Seizes her hand.]*

HELENA. Let go! *[She drags her hand away]* Go away!

VOITSKI. Soon the rain will be over, and all nature will sigh and awake refreshed. Only I am not refreshed by the storm. Day and night the thought haunts me like a fiend, that my life is lost for ever. My past does not count, because I frittered it away on trifles, and the present has so terribly miscarried! What shall I do with my life and my love? What is to become of them? This wonderful feeling of mine will be wasted and lost as a ray of sunlight is lost that falls into a dark chasm, and my life will go with it.

HELENA. I am as it were benumbed when you speak to me of your love, and I don't know how to answer you. Forgive me, I have nothing to say to you. *[She tries to go out]* Good-night!

VOITSKI. *[Barring the way]* If you only knew how I am tortured by the thought that beside me in this house is another life that is being lost forever—it is yours! What are you waiting for? What accursed philosophy stands in your way? Oh, understand, understand——

HELENA. *[Looking at him intently]* Ivan, you are drunk!

VOITSKI. Perhaps. Perhaps.

HELENA. Where is the doctor?

VOITSKI. In there, spending the night with me. Perhaps I am drunk, perhaps I am; nothing is impossible.

HELENA. Have you just been drinking together? Why do you do that?

VOITSKI. Because in that way I get a taste of life. Let me do it, Helena!

HELENA. You never used to drink, and you never used to talk so much. Go to bed, I am tired of you.

VOITSKI. *[Falling on his knees before her]* My sweetheart, my beautiful one——

HELENA. *[Angrily]* Leave me alone! Really, this has become too disagreeable.

[HELENA goes out. A pause.]

VOITSKI. *[Alone]* She is gone! I met her first ten years ago, at her sister's house, when she was seventeen and I was thirty-seven. Why did I not fall in love with her then and propose to her? It would have been so easy! And now she would have been my wife. Yes, we would both have been waked to-night by the thunderstorm, and she would have been frightened, but I would have held her in my arms and whispered: "Don't be afraid! I am here." Oh, enchanting dream, so sweet that I laugh to think of it. *[He laughs]* But my God! My head reels! Why am I so old? Why won't she understand me? I hate all that rhetoric of hers, that morality of indolence, that absurd talk about the destruction of the world——*[A pause]* Oh, how I have been deceived! For years I have worshipped that miserable gout-ridden professor. Sonia and I have squeezed this estate dry for his sake. We have bartered our butter and curds and peas like misers, and have never kept a morsel for ourselves, so that we could scrape enough pennies together to send to him. I was proud of him and of his learning; I received all his words and writings as inspired, and now? Now he has retired, and what is the total of his life? A blank! He is absolutely unknown, and his fame has burst like a soap-bubble. I have been deceived; I see that now, basely deceived.

[ASTROFF comes in. He has his coat on, but is without his waistcoat or collar, and is slightly drunk. TELEGIN follows him, carrying a guitar.]

ASTROFF. Play!

TELEGIN. But every one is asleep.

ASTROFF. Play!

[TELEGIN begins to play softly.]

ASTROFF. Are you alone here? No women about? *[Sings with his arms akimbo.]*

"The hut is cold, the fire is dead;
Where shall the master lay his head?"

The thunderstorm woke me. It was a heavy shower. What time is it?

VOITSKI. The devil only knows.

ASTROFF. I thought I heard Helena's voice.

VOITSKI. She was here a moment ago.

ASTROFF. What a beautiful woman! *[Looking at the medicine bottles on the table]* Medicine, is it? What a variety we have; prescriptions from Moscow, from Kharkoff, from Tula! Why, he has been pestering all the towns of Russia with his gout! Is he ill, or simply shamming?

VOITSKI. He is really ill.

ASTROFF. What is the matter with you to-night? You seem sad. Is it because you are sorry for the professor?

VOITSKI. Leave me alone.

ASTROFF. Or in love with the professor's wife?

VOITSKI. She is my friend.

ASTROFF. Already?

VOITSKI. What do you mean by "already"?

ASTROFF. A woman can only become a man's friend after having first been his acquaintance and then his beloved—then she becomes his friend.

VOITSKI. What vulgar philosophy!

ASTROFF. What do you mean? Yes, I must confess I am getting vulgar, but then, you see, I am drunk. I usually only drink like this once a month. At such times my audacity and temerity know no bounds. I feel capable of anything. I attempt the most difficult operations and do them magnificently. The most brilliant plans for the future take shape in my head. I am no longer a poor fool of a doctor, but mankind's greatest benefactor. I evolve my own system of philosophy and all of you seem to crawl at my feet like so many insects or microbes. *[To TELEGIN]* Play, Waffles!

TELEGIN. My dear boy, I would with all my heart, but do listen to reason; everybody in the house is asleep.

ASTROFF. Play!

[TELEGIN plays softly.]

ASTROFF. I want a drink. Come, we still have some brandy left. And then, as soon as it is day, you will come home with me. *[He sees SONIA, who comes in at that moment.]*

ASTROFF. I beg your pardon, I have no collar on.

[He goes out quickly, followed by TELEGIN.]

SONIA. Uncle Vanya, you and the doctor have been drinking! The good fellows have been getting together! It is all very well for him, he has always done it, but why do you follow his example? It looks dreadfully at your age.

VOITSKI. Age has nothing to do with it. When real life is wanting one must create an illusion. It is better than nothing.

SONIA. Our hay is all cut and rotting in these daily rains, and here you are busy creating illusions! You have given up the farm altogether. I have done all the work alone until I am at the end of my strength —*[Frightened]* Uncle! Your eyes are full of tears!

VOITSKI. Tears? Nonsense, there are no tears in my eyes. You looked at me then just as your dead mother used to, my darling—*[He eagerly kisses her face and hands]*

My sister, my dearest sister, where are you now? Ah, if you only knew, if you only knew!

SONIA. If she only knew what, Uncle?

VOITSKI. My heart is bursting. It is awful. No matter, though. I must go. *[He goes out.]*

SONIA. *[Knocks at the door]* Dr. Astroff! Are you awake? Please come here for a minute.

ASTROFF. *[Behind the door]* In a moment.

[He appears in a few seconds. He has put on his collar and waistcoat.]

ASTROFF. What do you want?

SONIA. Drink as much as you please yourself if you don't find it revolting, but I implore you not to let my uncle do it. It is bad for him.

ASTROFF. Very well; we won't drink any more. I am going home at once. That is settled. It will be dawn by the time the horses are harnessed.

SONIA. It is still raining; wait till morning.

ASTROFF. The storm is blowing over. This is only the edge of it. I must go. And please don't ask me to come and see your father any more. I tell him he has gout, and he says it is rheumatism. I tell him to lie down, and he sits up. To-day he refused to see me at all.

SONIA. He has been spoilt. *[She looks in the sideboard]* Won't you have a bite to eat?

ASTROFF. Yes, please. I believe I will.

SONIA. I love to eat at night. I am sure we shall find something in here. They say that he has made a great many conquests in his life, and that the women have spoiled him. Here is some cheese for you.

[They stand eating by the sideboard.]

ASTROFF. I haven't eaten anything to-day. Your father has a very difficult nature. *[He takes a bottle out of the sideboard]* May I? *[He pours himself a glass of vodka]* We are alone here, and I can speak frankly. Do you know, I could not stand living in this house for even a month? This atmosphere would stifle me. There is your father, entirely absorbed in his books, and his gout; there is your Uncle Vanya with his hypochondria, your grandmother, and finally, your step-mother—

SONIA. What about her?

ASTROFF. A human being should be entirely beautiful: the face, the clothes, the mind, the thoughts. Your step-mother is, of course, beautiful to look at, but don't you see? She does nothing but sleep and eat and walk and bewitch us, and that is all. She has no responsibilities, everything is done for her—am I not right? And an idle life can never be a pure one. *[A pause]* However, I may be judging her too severely. Like your Uncle Vanya, I am discontented, and so we are both grumblers.

SONIA. Aren't you satisfied with life?

ASTROFF. I like life as life, but I hate and despise it in a little Russian country village, and as far as my own personal life goes, by heaven! there is absolutely no redeeming feature about it. Haven't you noticed if you are riding through a dark wood at night and see a little light shining ahead, how you forget your fatigue and the darkness and the sharp twigs that whip your face? I work, that you know—as no one else in the country works. Fate beats me on without rest; at times I suffer unendurably and I see no light ahead. I have no hope; I do not like people. It is long since I have loved any one.

SONIA. You love no one?

ASTROFF. Not a soul. I only feel a sort of tenderness for your old nurse for old-times' sake. The peasants are all alike; they are stupid and live in dirt, and the educated people are hard to get along with. One gets

tired of them. All our good friends are petty and
shallow and see no farther than their own noses; in one
word, they are dull. Those that have brains are
hysterical, devoured with a mania for self-analysis.
They whine, they hate, they pick faults everywhere with
unhealthy sharpness. They sneak up to me sideways,
look at me out of a corner of the eye, and say: "That
man is a lunatic," "That man is a wind-bag." Or, if they
don't know what else to label me with, they say I am
strange. I like the woods; that is strange. I don't eat
meat; that is strange, too. Simple, natural relations
between man and man or man and nature do not exist.
[He tries to go out; SONIA prevents him.]

SONIA. I beg you, I implore you, not to drink any
more!

ASTROFF. Why not?

SONIA. It is so unworthy of you. You are well-bred,
your voice is sweet, you are even—more than any one I
know—handsome. Why do you want to resemble the
common people that drink and play cards? Oh, don't, I
beg you! You always say that people do not create
anything, but only destroy what heaven has given them.
Why, oh, why, do you destroy yourself? Oh, don't, I
implore you not to! I entreat you!

ASTROFF. *[Gives her his hand]* I won't drink any more.

SONIA. Promise me.

ASTROFF. I give you my word of honour.

SONIA. *[Squeezing his hand]* Thank you.

ASTROFF. I have done with it. You see, I am perfectly sober again, and so I shall stay till the end of my life. *[He looks his watch]* But, as I was saying, life holds nothing for me; my race is run. I am old, I am tired, I am trivial; my sensibilities are dead. I could never attach myself to any one again. I love no one, and never shall! Beauty alone has the power to touch me still. I am deeply moved by it. Helena could turn my head in a day if she wanted to, but that is not love, that is not affection—

[He shudders and covers his face with his hands.]

SONIA. What is it?

ASTROFF. Nothing. During Lent one of my patients died under chloroform.

SONIA. It is time to forget that. *[A pause]* Tell me, doctor, if I had a friend or a younger sister, and if you knew that she, well—loved you, what would you do?

ASTROFF. *[Shrugging his shoulders]* I don't know. I don't think I should do anything. I should make her understand that I could not return her love—however, my mind is not bothered about those things now. I must start at once if I am ever to get off. Good-bye, my dear girl. At this rate we shall stand here talking till morning. *[He shakes hands with her]* I shall go out through the sitting-room, because I am afraid your uncle might detain me. *[He goes out.]*

SONIA. *[Alone]* Not a word! His heart and soul are still locked from me, and yet for some reason I am strangely happy. I wonder why? *[She laughs with pleasure]* I told him that he was well-bred and handsome and that his voice was sweet. Was that a mistake? I can still feel his voice vibrating in the air; it caresses me. *[Wringing her hands]* Oh! how terrible it is to be plain! I am plain, I know it. As I came out of church last Sunday I overheard a woman say, "She is a dear, noble girl, but what a pity she is so ugly!" So ugly!

[HELENA comes in and throws open the window.]

HELENA. The storm is over. What delicious air! *[A pause]* Where is the doctor?

SONIA. He has gone. *[A pause.]*

HELENA. Sonia!

SONIA. Yes?

HELENA. How much longer are you going to sulk at me? We have not hurt each other. Why not be friends? We have had enough of this.

SONIA. I myself—*[She embraces HELENA]* Let us make peace.

HELENA. With all my heart. *[They are both moved.]*

SONIA. Has papa gone to bed?

HELENA. No, he is sitting up in the drawing-room. Heaven knows what reason you and I had for not speaking to each other for weeks. *[Sees the open sideboard]* Who left the sideboard open?

SONIA. Dr. Astroff has just had supper.

HELENA. There is some wine. Let us seal our friendship.

SONIA. Yes, let us.

HELENA. Out of one glass. *[She fills a wine-glass]* So, we are friends, are we?

SONIA. Yes. *[They drink and kiss each other]* I have long wanted to make friends, but somehow, I was ashamed to. *[She weeps.]*

HELENA. Why are you crying?

SONIA. I don't know. It is nothing.

HELENA. There, there, don't cry. *[She weeps]* Silly! Now I am crying too. *[A pause]* You are angry with me because I seem to have married your father for his money, but don't believe the gossip you hear. I swear to you I married him for love. I was fascinated by his fame and learning. I know now that it was not real love, but it seemed real at the time. I am innocent, and yet your clever, suspicious eyes have been punishing me for an imaginary crime ever since my marriage.

SONIA. Peace, peace! Let us forget the past.

HELENA. You must not look so at people. It is not becoming to you. You must trust people, or life becomes impossible.

SONIA. Tell me truly, as a friend, are you happy?

HELENA. Truly, no.

SONIA. I knew it. One more question: do you wish your husband were young?

HELENA. What a child you are! Of course I do. Go on, ask something else.

SONIA. Do you like the doctor?

HELENA. Yes, very much indeed.

SONIA. *[Laughing]* I have a stupid face, haven't I? He has just gone out, and his voice is still in my ears; I hear his step; I see his face in the dark window. Let me say all I have in my heart! But no, I cannot speak of it so loudly. I am ashamed. Come to my room and let me tell you there. I seem foolish to you, don't I? Talk to me of him.

HELENA. What can I say?

SONIA. He is clever. He can do everything. He can cure the sick, and plant woods.

HELENA. It is not a question of medicine and woods, my dear, he is a man of genius. Do you know what that means? It means he is brave, profound, and of clear insight. He plants a tree and his mind travels a thousand years into the future, and he sees visions of the happiness of the human race. People like him are rare and should be loved. What if he does drink and act roughly at times? A man of genius cannot be a saint in Russia. There he lives, cut off from the world by cold and storm and endless roads of bottomless mud, surrounded by a rough people who are crushed by poverty and disease, his life one continuous struggle, with never a day's respite; how can a man live like that for forty years and keep himself sober and unspotted? *[Kissing SONIA]* I wish you happiness with all my heart; you deserve it. *[She gets up]* As for me, I am a worthless, futile woman. I have always been futile; in music, in love, in my husband's house—in a word, in everything. When you come to think of it, Sonia, I am really very, very unhappy. *[Walks excitedly up and down]* Happiness can never exist for me in this world. Never. Why do you laugh?

SONIA. *[Laughing and covering her face with her hands]* I am so happy, so happy!

HELENA. I want to hear music. I might play a little.

SONIA. Oh, do, do! *[She embraces her]* I could not possibly go to sleep now. Do play!

HELENA. Yes, I will. Your father is still awake. Music irritates him when he is ill, but if he says I may, then I shall play a little. Go, Sonia, and ask him.

SONIA. Very well.

[She goes out. The WATCHMAN'S rattle is heard in the garden.]

HELENA. It is long since I have heard music. And now, I shall sit and play, and weep like a fool. *[Speaking out of the window]* Is that you rattling out there, Ephim?

VOICE OF THE WATCHMAN. It is I.

HELENA. Don't make such a noise. Your master is ill.

VOICE OF THE WATCHMAN. I am going away this minute. *[Whistles a tune.]*

SONIA. *[Comes back]* He says, no.

The curtain falls.

ACT III

[The drawing-room of SEREBRAKOFF'S house. There are three doors: one to the right, one to the left, and one in the centre of the room. VOITSKI and SONIA are sitting down. HELENA is walking up and down, absorbed in thought.]

VOITSKI. We were asked by the professor to be here at one o'clock. *[Looks at his watch]* It is now a quarter to one. It seems he has some communication to make to the world.

HELENA. Probably a matter of business.

VOITSKI. He never had any business. He writes twaddle, grumbles, and eats his heart out with jealousy; that's all he does.

SONIA. *[Reproachfully]* Uncle!

VOITSKI. All right. I beg your pardon. *[He points to HELENA]* Look at her. Wandering up and down from sheer idleness. A sweet picture, really.

HELENA. I wonder you are not bored, droning on in the same key from morning till night. *[Despairingly]* I am dying of this tedium. What shall I do?

SONIA. *[Shrugging her shoulders]* There is plenty to do if you would.

HELENA. For instance?

SONIA. You could help run this place, teach the children, care for the sick—isn't that enough? Before you and papa came, Uncle Vanya and I used to go to market ourselves to deal in flour.

HELENA. I don't know anything about such things, and besides, they don't interest me. It is only in novels that women go out and teach and heal the peasants; how can I suddenly begin to do it?

SONIA. How can you live here and not do it? Wait awhile, you will get used to it all. *[Embraces her]* Don't be sad, dearest. *[Laughing]* You feel miserable and restless, and can't seem to fit into this life, and your restlessness is catching. Look at Uncle Vanya, he does nothing now but haunt you like a shadow, and I have left my work to-day to come here and talk with you. I am getting lazy, and don't want to go on with it. Dr. Astroff hardly ever used to come here; it was all we could do to persuade him to visit us once a month, and now he has abandoned his forestry and his practice, and comes every day. You must be a witch.

VOITSKI. Why should you languish here? Come, my dearest, my beauty, be sensible! The blood of a Nixey runs in your veins. Oh, won't you let yourself be one? Give your nature the reins for once in your life; fall head over ears in love with some other water sprite and plunge down head first into a deep pool, so that the Herr Professor and all of us may have our hands free again.

HELENA. *[Angrily]* Leave me alone! How cruel you are! *[She tries to go out.]*

VOITSKI. *[Preventing her]* There, there, my beauty, I apologise. *[He kisses her hand]* Forgive me.

HELENA. Confess that you would try the patience of an angel.

VOITSKI. As a peace offering I am going to fetch some flowers which I picked for you this morning: some autumn roses, beautiful, sorrowful roses. *[He goes out.]*

SONIA. Autumn roses, beautiful, sorrowful roses!

[She and HELENA stand looking out of the window.]

HELENA. September already! How shall we live through the long winter here? *[A pause]* Where is the doctor?

SONIA. He is writing in Uncle Vanya's room. I am glad Uncle Vanya has gone out, I want to talk to you about something.

HELENA. About what?

SONIA. About what?

[She lays her head on HELENA'S breast.]

HELENA. *[Stroking her hair]* There, there, that will do. Don't, Sonia.

SONIA. I am ugly!

HELENA. You have lovely hair.

SONIA. Don't say that! *[She turns to look at herself in the glass]* No, when a woman is ugly they always say she has beautiful hair or eyes. I have loved him now for six years, I have loved him more than one loves one's mother. I seem to hear him beside me every moment of the day. I feel the pressure of his hand on mine. If I look up, I seem to see him coming, and as you see, I run to you to talk of him. He is here every day now, but he never looks at me, he does not notice my presence. It is agony. I have absolutely no hope, no, no hope. Oh, my God! Give me strength to endure. I prayed all last night. I often go up to him and speak to him and look into his eyes. My pride is gone. I am not mistress of myself. Yesterday I told Uncle Vanya I couldn't control myself, and all the servants know it. Every one knows that I love him.

HELENA. Does he?

SONIA. No, he never notices me.

HELENA. *[Thoughtfully]* He is a strange man. Listen, Sonia, will you allow me to speak to him? I shall be careful, only hint. *[A pause]* Really, to be in uncertainty all these years! Let me do it!

[SONIA nods an affirmative.]

HELENA. Splendid! It will be easy to find out whether he loves you or not. Don't be ashamed, sweetheart, don't worry. I shall be careful; he will not notice a thing. We only want to find out whether it is yes or no, don't we? *[A pause]* And if it is no, then he must keep away from here, is that so?

[SONIA nods.]

HELENA. It will be easier not to see him any more. We won't put off the examination an instant. He said he had a sketch to show me. Go and tell him at once that I want to see him.

SONIA. *[In great excitement]* Will you tell me the whole truth?

HELENA. Of course I will. I am sure that no matter what it is, it will be easier for you to bear than this uncertainty. Trust to me, dearest.

SONIA. Yes, yes. I shall say that you want to see his sketch. *[She starts out, but stops near the door and looks back]* No, it is better not to know—and yet—there may be hope.

HELENA. What do you say?

SONIA. Nothing. *[She goes out.]*

HELENA. *[Alone]* There is no greater sorrow than to know another's secret when you cannot help them. *[In deep thought]* He is obviously not in love with her, but why shouldn't he marry her? She is not pretty, but she is so clever and pure and good, she would make a splendid wife for a country doctor of his years. *[A pause]* I can understand how the poor child feels. She lives here in this desperate loneliness with no one around her except these colourless shadows that go mooning about talking nonsense and knowing nothing except that they eat, drink, and sleep. Among them appears from time to time this Dr. Astroff, so different, so handsome, so interesting, so charming. It is like seeing the moon rise on a dark night. Oh, to surrender oneself to his embrace! To lose oneself in his arms! I am a little in love with him myself! Yes, I am lonely without him, and when I think of him I smile. That Uncle Vanya says I have the blood of a Nixey in my veins: "Give rein to your nature for once in your life!" Perhaps it is right that I should. Oh, to be free as a bird, to fly away from all your sleepy faces and your talk and forget that you have existed at all! But I am a coward, I am afraid; my conscience torments me. He comes here every day now. I can guess why, and feel guilty already; I should like to fall on my knees at Sonia's feet and beg her forgiveness, and weep.

[ASTROFF comes in carrying a portfolio.]

ASTROFF. How do you do? *[Shakes hands with her]* Do you want to see my sketch?

HELENA. Yes, you promised to show me what you had been doing. Have you time now?

ASTROFF. Of course I have!

[He lays the portfolio on the table, takes out the sketch and fastens it to the table with thumb-tacks.]

ASTROFF. Where were you born?

HELENA. *[Helping him]* In St. Petersburg.

ASTROFF. And educated?

HELENA. At the Conservatory there.

ASTROFF. You don't find this life very interesting, I dare say?

HELENA. Oh, why not? It is true I don't know the country very well, but I have read a great deal about it.

ASTROFF. I have my own desk there in Ivan's room. When I am absolutely too exhausted to go on I drop everything and rush over here to forget myself in this work for an hour or two. Ivan and Miss Sonia sit rattling at their counting-boards, the cricket chirps, and I sit beside them and paint, feeling warm and peaceful. But I don't permit myself this luxury very often, only once a month. *[Pointing to the picture]* Look there! That is a map of our country as it was fifty years ago. The green tints, both dark and light, represent forests. Half the map, as you see, is covered with it. Where the green is striped with red the forests were inhabited by elk and wild goats. Here on this lake, lived great flocks of swans and geese and ducks; as the old men say, there was a power of birds of every kind. Now they have vanished like a cloud. Beside the hamlets and villages, you see, I have dotted down here and there the various settlements, farms, hermit's caves, and water-mills. This country carried a great many cattle and horses, as you can see by the quantity of blue paint. For instance, see how thickly it lies in this part; there were great herds of them here, an average of three horses to every house. *[A pause]* Now, look lower down. This is the country as it was twenty-five years ago. Only a third of the map is green now with forests. There are no goats left and no elk. The blue paint is lighter, and so on, and so on. Now we come to the third part; our country as it appears to-day. We still see spots of green, but not much. The elk, the swans, the black-cock have disappeared. It is, on the whole, the picture of a regular and slow decline which it will evidently only take about ten or fifteen more years to complete. You may perhaps object that it is the march of progress, that the old order must give place to the new, and you might be right if roads had been run through these ruined woods, or if factories and schools had taken their place. The people then would have become better educated and healthier and richer, but as it is, we have nothing of the sort. We have the same swamps and mosquitoes; the same disease and want; the typhoid, the diphtheria, the burning villages. We are confronted by the degradation of our country, brought on by the fierce struggle for existence of the human race. It is the consequence of the ignorance and unconsciousness of starving, shivering, sick humanity that, to save its children, instinctively snatches at everything that can warm it and still its hunger. So it destroys everything it can lay its hands on, without a thought for the morrow. And almost everything has gone, and nothing has been created to take its place. *[Coldly]* But I see by your face that I am not interesting you.

HELENA. I know so little about such things!

ASTROFF. There is nothing to know. It simply isn't interesting, that's all.

HELENA. Frankly, my thoughts were elsewhere. Forgive me! I want to submit you to a little examination, but I am embarrassed and don't know how to begin.

ASTROFF. An examination?

HELENA. Yes, but quite an innocent one. Sit down. *[They sit down]* It is about a certain young girl I know.

Let us discuss it like honest people, like friends, and then forget what has passed between us, shall we?

ASTROFF. Very well.

HELENA. It is about my step-daughter, Sonia. Do you like her?

ASTROFF. Yes, I respect her.

HELENA. Do you like her—as a woman?

ASTROFF. *[Slowly]* No.

HELENA. One more word, and that will be the last. You have not noticed anything?

ASTROFF. No, nothing.

HELENA. *[Taking his hand]* You do not love her. I see that in your eyes. She is suffering. You must realise that, and not come here any more.

ASTROFF. My sun has set, yes, and then I haven't the time. *[Shrugging his shoulders]* Where shall I find time for such things? *[He is embarrassed.]*

HELENA. Bah! What an unpleasant conversation! I am as out of breath as if I had been running three miles uphill. Thank heaven, that is over! Now let us forget everything as if nothing had been said. You are sensible. You understand. *[A pause]* I am actually blushing.

ASTROFF. If you had spoken a month ago I might perhaps have considered it, but now—*[He shrugs his shoulders]* Of course, if she is suffering—but I cannot understand why you had to put me through this examination. *[He searches her face with his eyes, and shakes his finger at her]* Oho, you are wily!

HELENA. What does this mean?

ASTROFF. *[Laughing]* You are a wily one! I admit that Sonia is suffering, but what does this examination of yours mean? *[He prevents her from retorting, and goes on quickly]* Please don't put on such a look of surprise; you know perfectly well why I come here every day. Yes, you know perfectly why and for whose sake I come! Oh, my sweet tigress! don't look at me in that way; I am an old bird!

HELENA. *[Perplexed]* A tigress? I don't understand you.

ASTROFF. Beautiful, sleek tigress, you must have your victims! For a whole month I have done nothing but seek you eagerly. I have thrown over everything for you, and you love to see it. Now then, I am sure you knew all this without putting me through your examination.

[Crossing his arms and bowing his head] I surrender. Here you have me—now, eat me.

HELENA. You have gone mad!

ASTROFF. You are afraid!

HELENA. I am a better and stronger woman than you think me. Good-bye. *[She tries to leave the room.]*

ASTROFF. Why good-bye? Don't say good-bye, don't waste words. Oh, how lovely you are—what hands! *[He kisses her hands.]*

HELENA. Enough of this! *[She frees her hands]* Leave the room! You have forgotten yourself.

ASTROFF. Tell me, tell me, where can we meet to-morrow? *[He puts his arm around her]* Don't you see that we must meet, that it is inevitable?

[He kisses her. VOITSKI comes in carrying a bunch of roses, and stops in the doorway.]

HELENA. *[Without seeing VOITSKI]* Have pity! Leave me, *[lays her head on ASTROFF'S shoulder]* Don't! *[She tries to break away from him.]*

ASTROFF. *[Holding her by the waist]* Be in the forest tomorrow at two o'clock. Will you? Will you?

HELENA. *[Sees VOITSKI]* Let me go! *[Goes to the window deeply embarrassed]* This is appalling!

VOITSKI. *[Throws the flowers on a chair, and speaks in great excitement, wiping his face with his handkerchief]* Nothing— yes, yes, nothing.

ASTROFF. The weather is fine to-day, my dear Ivan; the morning was overcast and looked like rain, but now the sun is shining again. Honestly, we have had a very fine autumn, and the wheat is looking fairly well. *[Puts his map back into the portfolio]* But the days are growing short.

HELENA. *[Goes quickly up to VOITSKI]* You must do your best; you must use all your power to get my husband and myself away from here to-day! Do you hear? I say, this very day!

VOITSKI. *[Wiping his face]* Oh! Ah! Oh! All right! I— Helena, I saw everything!

HELENA. *[In great agitation]* Do you hear me? I must leave here this very day!

SEREBRAKOFF, SONIA, MARINA, and TELEGIN come in.

TELEGIN. I am not very well myself, your Excellency. I have been limping for two days, and my head—

SEREBRAKOFF. Where are the others? I hate this house. It is a regular labyrinth. Every one is always scattered through the twenty-six enormous rooms; one never can find a soul. *[Rings]* Ask my wife and Madame Voitskaya to come here!

HELENA. I am here already.

SEREBRAKOFF. Please, all of you, sit down.

SONIA. *[Goes up to HELENA and asks anxiously]* What did he say?

HELENA. I'll tell you later.

SONIA. You are moved. *[looking quickly and inquiringly into her face]* I understand; he said he would not come here any more. *[A pause]* Tell me, did he?

[HELENA nods.]

SEREBRAKOFF. *[To TELEGIN]* One can, after all, become reconciled to being an invalid, but not to this country life. The ways of it stick in my throat and I feel exactly as if I had been whirled off the earth and landed on a strange planet. Please be seated, ladies and gentlemen. Sonia! *[SONIA does not hear. She is standing with her head bowed sadly forward on her breast]* Sonia! *[A pause]* She does not hear me. *[To MARINA]* Sit down too, nurse. *[MARINA sits down and begins to knit her *stocking]* I crave your indulgence, ladies and gentlemen; hang your ears, if I may say so, on the peg of attention. *[He laughs.]*

VOITSKI. *[Agitated]* Perhaps you do not need me—may I be excused?

SEREBRAKOFF. No, you are needed now more than any one.

VOITSKI. What is it you want of me?

SEREBRAKOFF. You—but what are you angry about? If it is anything I have done, I ask you to forgive me.

VOITSKI. Oh, drop that and come to business; what do you want?

[MME. VOITSKAYA comes in.]

SEREBRAKOFF. Here is mother. Ladies and gentlemen, I shall begin. I have asked you to assemble here, my friends, in order to discuss a very important matter. I want to ask you for your assistance and advice, and knowing your unfailing amiability I think I can count on both. I am a book-worm and a scholar, and am unfamiliar with practical affairs. I cannot, I find, dispense with the help of well-informed people such as you, Ivan, and you, Telegin, and you, mother. The truth is, *manet omnes una nox,* that is to say, our lives are in the hands of God, and as I am old and ill, I realise that the time has come for me to dispose of my property in regard to the interests of my family. My life is nearly over, and I am not thinking of myself, but I have a young wife and daughter. *[A pause]* I cannot continue to live in the country; we were not made for country life, and yet we cannot afford to live in town on the income derived from this estate. We might sell the woods, but that would be an expedient we could not resort to every year. We must find some means of guaranteeing to ourselves a certain more or less fixed yearly income. With this object in view, a plan has occurred to me which I now have the honour of presenting to you for your consideration. I shall only give you a rough outline, avoiding all details. Our estate does not pay on an average more than two per cent on the money invested in it. I propose to sell it. If we then invest our capital in bonds, it will earn us four to five per cent, and we should probably have a surplus over of several thousand roubles, with which we could buy a summer cottage in Finland—

VOITSKI. Hold on! Repeat what you just said; I don't think I heard you quite right.

SEREBRAKOFF. I said we would invest the money in bonds and buy a cottage in Finland with the surplus.

VOITSKI. No, not Finland—you said something else.

SEREBRAKOFF. I propose to sell this place.

VOITSKI. Aha! That was it! So you are going to sell the place? Splendid. The idea is a rich one. And what do you propose to do with my old mother and me and with Sonia here?

SEREBRAKOFF. That will be decided in due time. We can't do everything at once.

VOITSKI. Wait! It is clear that until this moment I have never had a grain of sense in my head. I have always been stupid enough to think that the estate belonged to Sonia. My father bought it as a wedding present for my sister, and I foolishly imagined that as our laws were made for Russians and not Turks, my sister's estate would come down to her child.

SEREBRAKOFF. Of course it is Sonia's. Has any one denied it? I don't want to sell it without Sonia's consent; on the contrary, what I am doing is for Sonia's good.

VOITSKI. This is absolutely incomprehensible. Either I have gone mad or—or—

MME. VOITSKAYA. Jean, don't contradict Alexander. Trust to him; he knows better than we do what is right and what is wrong.

VOITSKI. I shan't. Give me some water. *[He drinks]* Go ahead! Say anything you please—anything!

SEREBRAKOFF. I can't imagine why you are so upset. I don't pretend that my scheme is an ideal one, and if you all object to it I shall not insist. *[A pause.]*

TELEGIN. *[With embarrassment]* I not only nourish feelings of respect toward learning, your Excellency, but I am also drawn to it by family ties. My brother Gregory's wife's brother, whom you may know; his name is Constantine Lakedemonoff, and he used to be a magistrate—

VOITSKI. Stop, Waffles. This is business; wait a bit, we will talk of that later. *[To SEREBRAKOFF]* There now, ask him what he thinks; this estate was bought from his uncle.

SEREBRAKOFF. Ah! Why should I ask questions? What good would it do?

VOITSKI. The price was ninety-five thousand roubles. My father paid seventy and left a debt of twenty-five. Now listen! This place could never have been bought had I not renounced my inheritance in favour of my sister, whom I deeply loved—and what is more, I worked for ten years like an ox, and paid off the debt.

SEREBRAKOFF. I regret ever having started this conversation.

VOITSKI. Thanks entirely to my own personal efforts, the place is entirely clear of debts, and now, when I have grown old, you want to throw me out, neck and crop!

SEREBRAKOFF. I can't imagine what you are driving at.

VOITSKI. For twenty-five years I have managed this place, and have sent you the returns from it like the most honest of servants, and you have never given me one single word of thanks for my work, not one— neither in my youth nor now. You allowed me a meagre salary of five hundred roubles a year, a beggar's pittance, and have never even thought of adding a rouble to it.

SEREBRAKOFF. What did I know about such things, Ivan? I am not a practical man and don't understand them. You might have helped yourself to all you wanted.

VOITSKI. Yes, why did I not steal? Don't you all despise me for not stealing, when it would have been only justice? And I should not now have been a beggar!

MME. VOITSKAYA. *[Sternly]* Jean!

TELEGIN. *[Agitated]* Vanya, old man, don't talk in that way. Why spoil such pleasant relations? *[He embraces him]* Do stop!

VOITSKI. For twenty-five years I have been sitting here with my mother like a mole in a burrow. Our every thought and hope was yours and yours only. By day we talked with pride of you and your work, and spoke your name with veneration; our nights we wasted reading the books and papers which my soul now loathes.

TELEGIN. Don't, Vanya, don't. I can't stand it.

SEREBRAKOFF. *[Wrathfully]* What under heaven do you want, anyway?

VOITSKI. We used to think of you as almost superhuman, but now the scales have fallen from my eyes and I see you as you are! You write on art without knowing anything about it. Those books of yours which I used to admire are not worth one copper kopeck. You are a hoax!

SEREBRAKOFF. Can't any one make him stop? I am going!

HELENA. Ivan, I command you to stop this instant! Do you hear me?

VOITSKI. I refuse! [*SEREBRAKOFF tries to get out of the room, but VOITSKI bars the door*] Wait! I have not done yet! You have wrecked my life. I have never lived. My best years have gone for nothing, have been ruined, thanks to you. You are my most bitter enemy!

TELEGIN. I can't stand it; I can't stand it. I am going. [*He goes out in great excitement.*]

SEREBRAKOFF. But what do you want? What earthly right have you to use such language to me? Ruination! If this estate is yours, then take it, and let me be ruined!

HELENA. I am going away out of this hell this minute. [*Shrieks*] This is too much!

VOITSKI. My life has been a failure. I am clever and brave and strong. If I had lived a normal life I might have become another Schopenhauer or Dostoieffski. I am losing my head! I am going crazy! Mother, I am in despair! Oh, mother!

MME. VOITSKAYA. [*Sternly*] Listen, Alexander!

[SONIA falls on her knees beside the nurse and nestles against her.]

SONIA. Oh, nurse, nurse!

VOITSKI. Mother! What shall I do? But no, don't speak! I know what to do. *[To SEREBRAKOFF]* And you will understand me!

[He goes out through the door in the centre of the room and MME. VOITSKAYA follows him.]

SEREBRAKOFF. Tell me, what on earth is the matter? Take this lunatic out of my sight! I cannot possibly live under the same roof with him. His room *[He points to the centre door]* is almost next door to mine. Let him take himself off into the village or into the wing of the house, or I shall leave here at once. I cannot stay in the same house with him.

HELENA. *[To her husband]* We are leaving to-day; we must get ready at once for our departure.

SEREBRAKOFF. What a perfectly dreadful man!

SONIA. *[On her knees beside the nurse and turning to her father. She speaks with emotion]* You must be kind to us, papa. Uncle Vanya and I are so unhappy! *[Controlling her despair]* Have pity on us. Remember how Uncle Vanya and Granny used to copy and translate your books for you every night—every, every night. Uncle Vanya has toiled without rest; he would never spend a penny on us, we sent it all to you. We have not eaten the bread of idleness. I am not saying this as I should like to, but you must understand us, papa, you must be merciful to us.

HELENA. *[Very excited, to her husband]* For heaven's sake, Alexander, go and have a talk with him—explain!

SEREBRAKOFF. Very well, I shall have a talk with him, but I won't apologise for a thing. I am not angry with him, but you must confess that his behaviour has been strange, to say the least. Excuse me, I shall go to him.

[He goes out through the centre door.]

HELENA. Be gentle with him; try to quiet him. *[She follows him out.]*

SONIA. *[Nestling nearer to MARINA]* Nurse, oh, nurse!

MARINA. It's all right, my baby. When the geese have cackled they will be still again. First they cackle and then they stop.

SONIA. Nurse!

MARINA. You are trembling all over, as if you were freezing. There, there, little orphan baby, God is

merciful. A little linden-tea, and it will all pass away.
Don't cry, my sweetest. *[Looking angrily at the door in the
centre of the room]* See, the geese have all gone now. The
devil take them!

*[A shot is heard. HELENA screams behind the scenes. SONIA
shudders.]*

MARINA. Bang! What's that?

SEREBRAKOFF. *[Comes in reeling with terror]* Hold him!
hold him! He has gone mad!

HELENA and VOITSKI are seen struggling in the
doorway.

HELENA. *[Trying to wrest the revolver from him]* Give it to
me; give it to me, I tell you!

VOITSKI. Let me go, Helena, let me go! *[He frees
himself and rushes in, looking everywhere for SEREBRAKOFF]*
Where is he? Ah, there he is! *[He shoots at him. A pause]* I
didn't get him? I missed again? *[Furiously]* Damnation!
Damnation! To hell with him!

*[He flings the revolver on the floor, and drops helpless into a chair.
SEREBRAKOFF stands as if stupefied. HELENA leans
against the wall, almost fainting.]*

HELENA. Take me away! Take me away! I can't stay here—I can't!

VOITSKI. *[In despair]* Oh, what shall I do? What shall I do?

SONIA. *[Softly]* Oh, nurse, nurse!

The curtain falls.

ACT IV

[VOITSKI'S bedroom, which is also his office. A table stands near the window; on it are ledgers, letter scales, and papers of every description. Near by stands a smaller table belonging to ASTROFF, with his paints and drawing materials. On the wall hangs a cage containing a starling. There is also a map of Africa on the wall, obviously of no use to anybody. There is a large sofa covered with buckram. A door to the left leads into an inner room; one to the right leads into the front hall, and before this door lies a mat for the peasants with their muddy boots to stand on. It is an autumn evening. The silence is profound. TELEGIN and MARINA are sitting facing one another, winding wool.]

TELEGIN. Be quick, Marina, or we shall be called away to say good-bye before you have finished. The carriage has already been ordered.

MARINA. *[Trying to wind more quickly]* I am a little tired.

TELEGIN. They are going to Kharkoff to live.

MARINA. They do well to go.

TELEGIN. They have been frightened. The professor's wife won't stay here an hour longer. "If we are going at all, let's be off," says she, "we shall go to Kharkoff and look about us, and then we can send for our things." They are travelling light. It seems, Marina, that fate has decreed for them not to live here.

MARINA. And quite rightly. What a storm they have just raised! It was shameful!

TELEGIN. It was indeed. The scene was worthy of the brush of Aibazofski.

MARINA. I wish I'd never laid eyes on them. *[A pause]* Now we shall have things as they were again: tea at eight, dinner at one, and supper in the evening; everything in order as decent folks, as Christians like to have it. *[Sighs]* It is a long time since I have eaten noodles.

TELEGIN. Yes, we haven't had noodles for ages. *[A pause]* Not for ages. As I was going through the village this morning, Marina, one of the shop-keepers called after me, "Hi! you hanger-on!" I felt it bitterly.

MARINA. Don't pay the least attention to them, master; we are all dependents on God. You and Sonia and all of us. Every one must work, no one can sit idle. Where is Sonia?

TELEGIN. In the garden with the doctor, looking for Ivan. They fear he may lay violent hands on himself.

MARINA. Where is his pistol?

TELEGIN. *[Whispers]* I hid it in the cellar.

[VOITSKI and ASTROFF come in.]

VOITSKI. Leave me alone! *[To MARINA and TELEGIN]* Go away! Go away and leave me to myself, if but for an hour. I won't have you watching me like this!

TELEGIN. Yes, yes, Vanya. *[He goes out on tiptoe.]*

MARINA. The gander cackles; ho! ho! ho!

[She gathers up her wool and goes out.]

VOITSKI. Leave me by myself!

ASTROFF. I would, with the greatest pleasure. I ought to have gone long ago, but I shan't leave you until you have returned what you took from me.

VOITSKI. I took nothing from you.

ASTROFF. I am not jesting, don't detain me, I really must go.

VOITSKI. I took nothing of yours.

ASTROFF. You didn't? Very well, I shall have to wait a little longer, and then you will have to forgive me if I resort to force. We shall have to bind you and search you. I mean what I say.

VOITSKI. Do as you please. *[A pause]* Oh, to make such a fool of myself! To shoot twice and miss him both times! I shall never forgive myself.

ASTROFF. When the impulse came to shoot, it would have been as well had you put a bullet through your own head.

VOITSKI. *[Shrugging his shoulders]* Strange! I attempted murder, and am not going to be arrested or brought to trial. That means they think me mad. *[With a bitter laugh]* Me! I am mad, and those who hide their worthlessness, their dullness, their crying heartlessness behind a professor's mask, are sane! Those who marry old men and then deceive them under the noses of all, are sane! I saw you kiss her; I saw you in each other's arms!

ASTROFF. Yes, sir, I did kiss her; so there. *[He puts his thumb to his nose.]*

VOITSKI. *[His eyes on the door]* No, it is the earth that is mad, because she still bears us on her breast.

ASTROFF. That is nonsense.

VOITSKI. Well? Am I not a madman, and therefore irresponsible? Haven't I the right to talk nonsense?

ASTROFF. This is a farce! You are not mad; you are simply a ridiculous fool. I used to think every fool was out of his senses, but now I see that lack of sense is a man's normal state, and you are perfectly normal.

VOITSKI. *[Covers his face with his hands]* Oh! If you knew how ashamed I am! These piercing pangs of shame are like nothing on earth. *[In an agonised voice]* I can't endure them! *[He leans against the table]* What can I do? What can I do?

ASTROFF. Nothing.

VOITSKI. You must tell me something! Oh, my God! I am forty-seven years old. I may live to sixty; I still have thirteen years before me; an eternity! How shall I be able to endure life for thirteen years? What shall I do? How can I fill them? Oh, don't you see? *[He presses ASTROFF'S hand convulsively]* Don't you see, if only I

could live the rest of my life in some new way! If I
could only wake some still, bright morning and feel that
life had begun again; that the past was forgotten and
had vanished like smoke. *[He weeps]* Oh, to begin life
anew! Tell me, tell me how to begin.

ASTROFF. *[Crossly]* What nonsense! What sort of a
new life can you and I look forward to? We can have no
hope.

VOITSKI. None?

ASTROFF. None. Of that I am convinced.

VOITSKI. Tell me what to do. *[He puts his hand to his
heart]* I feel such a burning pain here.

ASTROFF. *[Shouts angrily]* Stop! *[Then, more gently]* It
may be that posterity, which will despise us for our
blind and stupid lives, will find some road to happiness;
but we—you and I—have but one hope, the hope that
we may be visited by visions, perhaps by pleasant ones,
as we lie resting in our graves. *[Sighing]* Yes, brother,
there were only two respectable, intelligent men in this
county, you and I. Ten years or so of this life of ours,
this miserable life, have sucked us under, and we have
become as contemptible and petty as the rest. But don't
try to talk me out of my purpose! Give me what you
took from me, will you?

VOITSKI. I took nothing from you.

ASTROFF. You took a little bottle of morphine out of my medicine-case. *[A pause]* Listen! If you are positively determined to make an end to yourself, go into the woods and shoot yourself there. Give up the morphine, or there will be a lot of talk and guesswork; people will think I gave it to you. I don't fancy having to perform a post-mortem on you. Do you think I should find it interesting?

[SONIA comes in.]

VOITSKI. Leave me alone.

ASTROFF. *[To SONIA]* Sonia, your uncle has stolen a bottle of morphine out of my medicine-case and won't give it up. Tell him that his behaviour is—well, unwise. I haven't time, I must be going.

SONIA. Uncle Vanya, did you take the morphine?

ASTROFF. Yes, he took it. *[A pause]* I am absolutely sure.

SONIA. Give it up! Why do you want to frighten us? *[Tenderly]* Give it up, Uncle Vanya! My misfortune is perhaps even greater than yours, but I am not plunged in despair. I endure my sorrow, and shall endure it until my life comes to a natural end. You must endure yours, too. *[A pause]* Give it up! Dear, darling Uncle Vanya. Give it up! *[She weeps]* You are so good, I am sure you will have pity on us and give it up. You must endure your sorrow, Uncle Vanya; you must endure it.

[VOITSKI takes a bottle from the drawer of the table and hands it to ASTROFF.]

VOITSKI. There it is! *[To SONIA]* And now, we must get to work at once; we must do something, or else I shall not be able to endure it.

SONIA. Yes, yes, to work! As soon as we have seen them off we shall go to work. *[She nervously straightens out the papers on the table]* Everything is in a muddle!

ASTROFF. *[Putting the bottle in his case, which he straps together]* Now I can be off.

[HELENA comes in.]

HELENA. Are you here, Ivan? We are starting in a moment. Go to Alexander, he wants to speak to you.

SONIA. Go, Uncle Vanya. *[She takes VOITSKI 'S arm]* Come, you and papa must make peace; that is absolutely necessary.

[SONIA and VOITSKI go out.]

HELENA. I am going away. *[She gives ASTROFF her hand]* Good-bye.

ASTROFF. So soon?

HELENA. The carriage is waiting.

ASTROFF. Good-bye.

HELENA. You promised me you would go away yourself to-day.

ASTROFF. I have not forgotten. I am going at once. *[A pause]* Were you frightened? Was it so terrible?

HELENA. Yes.

ASTROFF. Couldn't you stay? Couldn't you? To-morrow—in the forest—

HELENA. No. It is all settled, and that is why I can look you so bravely in the face. Our departure is fixed. One thing I must ask of you: don't think too badly of me; I should like you to respect me.

ASTROFF. Ah! *[With an impatient gesture]* Stay, I implore you! Confess that there is nothing for you to do in this world. You have no object in life; there is nothing to occupy your attention, and sooner or later your feelings must master you. It is inevitable. It would be better if it happened not in Kharkoff or in Kursk, but here, in nature's lap. It would then at least be poetical, even beautiful. Here you have the forests, the houses half in ruins that Turgenieff writes of.

HELENA. How comical you are! I am angry with you and yet I shall always remember you with pleasure. You are interesting and original. You and I will never meet again, and so I shall tell you—why should I conceal it? —that I am just a little in love with you. Come, one more last pressure of our hands, and then let us part good friends. Let us not bear each other any ill will.

ASTROFF. *[Pressing her hand]* Yes, go. *[Thoughtfully]* You seem to be sincere and good, and yet there is something strangely disquieting about all your personality. No sooner did you arrive here with your husband than every one whom you found busy and actively creating something was forced to drop his work and give himself up for the whole summer to your husband's gout and yourself. You and he have infected us with your idleness. I have been swept off my feet; I have not put my hand to a thing for weeks, during which sickness has been running its course unchecked among the people, and the peasants have been pasturing their cattle in my woods and young plantations. Go where you will, you and your husband will always carry destruction in your train. I am joking of course, and yet I am strangely sure that had you stayed here we should have been overtaken by the most immense desolation. I would have gone to my ruin, and you—you would not have prospered. So go! E finita la comedia!

HELENA. *[Snatching a pencil off ASTROFF'S table, and hiding it with a quick movement]* I shall take this pencil for memory!

ASTROFF. How strange it is. We meet, and then suddenly it seems that we must part forever. That is the way in this world. As long as we are alone, before Uncle Vanya comes in with a bouquet—allow me—to kiss you good-bye—may I? *[He kisses her on the cheek]* So! Splendid!

HELENA. I wish you every happiness. *[She glances about her]* For once in my life, I shall! and scorn the consequences! *[She kisses him impetuously, and they quickly part]* I must go.

ASTROFF. Yes, go. If the carriage is there, then start at once. *[They stand listening.]*

ASTROFF. E finita!

[VOITSKI, SEREBRAKOFF, MME. VOITSKAYA with her book, TELEGIN, and SONIA come in.]

SEREBRAKOFF. *[To VOITSKI]* Shame on him who bears malice for the past. I have gone through so much in the last few hours that I feel capable of writing a whole treatise on the conduct of life for the instruction of posterity. I gladly accept your apology, and myself ask your forgiveness. *[He kisses VOITSKI three times.]*

[HELENA embraces SONIA.]

SEREBRAKOFF. *[Kissing MME. VOITSKAYA'S hand]* Mother!

MME. VOITSKAYA. *[Kissing him]* Have your picture taken, Alexander, and send me one. You know how dear you are to me.

TELEGIN. Good-bye, your Excellency. Don't forget us.

SEREBRAKOFF. *[Kissing his daughter]* Good-bye, good-bye all. *[Shaking hands with ASTROFF]* Many thanks for your pleasant company. I have a deep regard for your opinions and your enthusiasm, but let me, as an old man, give one word of advice at parting: do something, my friend! Work! Do something! *[They all bow]* Good luck to you all. *[He goes out followed by MME. VOITSKAYA and SONIA.]*

VOITSKI *[Kissing HELENA'S hand fervently]* Good-bye —forgive me. I shall never see you again!

HELENA. *[Touched]* Good-bye, dear boy.

[She lightly kisses his head as he bends over her hand, and goes out.]

ASTROFF. Tell them to bring my carriage around too, Waffles.

TELEGIN. All right, old man.

ASTROFF and VOITSKI are left behind alone. ASTROFF collects his paints and drawing materials on the table and packs them away in a box.

ASTROFF. Why don't you go to see them off?

VOITSKI. Let them go! I—I can't go out there. I feel too sad. I must go to work on something at once. To work! To work!

[He rummages through his papers on the table. A pause. The tinkling of bells is heard as the horses trot away.]

ASTROFF. They have gone! The professor, I suppose, is glad to go. He couldn't be tempted back now by a fortune.

MARINA comes in.

MARINA. They have gone. *[She sits down in an arm-chair and knits her stocking.]*

[SONIA comes in wiping her eyes.]

SONIA. They have gone. God be with them. *[To her uncle]* And now, Uncle Vanya, let us do something!

VOITSKI. To work! To work!

SONIA. It is long, long, since you and I have sat together at this table. *[She lights a lamp on the table]* No ink! *[She takes the inkstand to the cupboard and fills it from an ink-bottle]* How sad it is to see them go!

MME. VOITSKAYA comes slowly in.

MME. VOITSKAYA. They have gone.

[She sits down and at once becomes absorbed in her book. SONIA sits down at the table and looks through an account book.]

SONIA. First, Uncle Vanya, let us write up the accounts. They are in a dreadful state. Come, begin. You take one and I will take the other.

VOITSKI. In account with *[They sit silently writing.]*

MARINA. *[Yawning]* The sand-man has come.

ASTROFF. How still it is. Their pens scratch, the cricket sings; it is so warm and comfortable. I hate to go. *[The tinkling of bells is heard.]*

ASTROFF. My carriage has come. There now remains but to say good-bye to you, my friends, and to my table here, and then—away! *[He puts the map into the portfolio.]*

MARINA. Don't hurry away; sit a little longer with us.

ASTROFF. Impossible.

VOITSKI. *[Writing]* And carry forward from the old debt two seventy-five—

[WORKMAN comes in.]

WORKMAN. Your carriage is waiting, sir.

ASTROFF. All right. *[He hands the WORKMAN his medicine-case, portfolio, and box]* Look out, don't crush the portfolio!

WORKMAN. Very well, sir.

SONIA. When shall we see you again?

ASTROFF. Hardly before next summer. Probably not this winter, though, of course, if anything should happen you will let me know. *[He shakes hands with them]* Thank you for your kindness, for your hospitality, for everything! *[He goes up to MARINA and kisses her head]* Good-bye, old nurse!

MARINA. Are you going without your tea?

ASTROFF. I don't want any, nurse.

MARINA. Won't you have a drop of vodka?

ASTROFF. *[Hesitatingly]* Yes, I might.

MARINA goes out.

ASTROFF. *[After a pause]* My off-wheeler has gone lame for some reason. I noticed it yesterday when Peter was taking him to water.

VOITSKI. You should have him re-shod.

ASTROFF. I shall have to go around by the blacksmith's on my way home. It can't be avoided. *[He stands looking up at the map of Africa hanging on the wall]* I suppose it is roasting hot in Africa now.

VOITSKI. Yes, I suppose it is.

MARINA comes back carrying a tray on which are a glass of vodka and a piece of bread.

MARINA. Help yourself.

[ASTROFF drinks]

MARINA. To your good health! *[She bows deeply]* Eat your bread with it.

ASTROFF. No, I like it so. And now, good-bye. *[To MARINA]* You needn't come out to see me off, nurse.

[He goes out. SONIA follows him with a candle to light him to the carriage. MARINA sits down in her armchair.]

VOITSKI. *[Writing]* On the 2d of February, twenty pounds of butter; on the 16th, twenty pounds of butter again. Buckwheat flour—*[A pause. Bells are heard tinkling.]*

MARINA. He has gone. *[A pause.]*

[SONIA comes in and sets the candle stick on the table.]

SONIA. He has gone.

VOITSKI. *[Adding and writing]* Total, fifteen—twenty-five—

[SONIA sits down and begins to write.]

[Yawning] Oh, ho! The Lord have mercy.

[TELEGIN comes in on tiptoe, sits down near the door, and begins to tune his guitar.]

VOITSKI. *[To SONIA, stroking her hair]* Oh, my child, I am miserable; if you only knew how miserable I am!

SONIA. What can we do? We must live our lives. *[A pause]* Yes, we shall live, Uncle Vanya. We shall live through the long procession of days before us, and through the long evenings; we shall patiently bear the trials that fate imposes on us; we shall work for others without rest, both now and when we are old; and when our last hour comes we shall meet it humbly, and there, beyond the grave, we shall say that we have suffered and wept, that our life was bitter, and God will have pity on us. Ah, then dear, dear Uncle, we shall see that bright and beautiful life; we shall rejoice and look back upon our sorrow here; a tender smile—and—we shall rest. I have faith, Uncle, fervent, passionate faith. *[SONIA kneels down before her uncle and lays her head on his hands. She speaks in a weary voice]* We shall rest. *[TELEGIN plays softly on the guitar]* We shall rest. We shall hear the angels. We shall see heaven shining like a jewel. We shall see all evil and all our pain sink away in the great compassion that shall enfold the world. Our life will be as peaceful and tender and sweet as a caress. I have faith; I have faith. *[She wipes away her tears]* My poor, poor Uncle Vanya, you are crying! *[Weeping]* You have never known what happiness was, but wait, Uncle Vanya, wait! We shall rest. *[She embraces him]* We shall rest. *[The WATCHMAN'S rattle is heard in the garden; TELEGIN plays softly; MME. VOITSKAYA writes something on the margin of her pamphlet; MARINA knits her stocking]* We shall rest.

The curtain slowly falls.

Made in the USA
Las Vegas, NV
07 June 2021